TYPOGRAPHY FOR THE PEOPLE

Hand-Painted Signs From Around the World

Kowloon, Hong Kong

TYPOGRAPHY FOR THE PEOPLE

Hand-Painted Signs From Around the World

Daniel Bellon and Klaus Bellon

HOW
BOOKS
Cincinnati, Ohio
www.howdesign.com

TYPOGRAPHY FOR THE PEOPLE

For more excellent books and resources for designers, visit www.howdesign.com.

14 13 12 11 10   5 4 3 2 1

Distributed in Canada by Fraser Direct
100 Armstrong Avenue
Georgetown, Ontario, Canada L7G 5S4
Tel: (905) 877-4411

Distributed in the U.K. and
Europe by David & Charles
Brunel House, Newton Abbot, Devon,
TQ12 4PU, England
Tel: (+44) 1626-323200, Fax: (+44) 1626-323319
E-mail: postmaster@davidandcharles.co.uk

Distributed in Australia by Capricorn Link
P.O. Box 704, Windsor, NSW 2756 Australia
Tel: (02) 4577-3555

Library of Congress Cataloging-in-Publication Data

Bellon, Daniel.
  Typography for the people : hand-painted signs from around the world / Daniel Bellon and Klaus Bellon.
      p. cm.
  Includes index.
  ISBN 978-1-60061-464-4 (hardcover : alk. paper)
  1. Signs and signboards--Lettering. 2. Painted signs and signboards. I. Bellon, Klaus. II. Title.
  NK3630.3.S54B45 2010
  760--dc22
                          2010006736

Edited by Amy Schell Owen
Designed by Daniel Bellon and Klaus Bellon
Art directed by Grace Ring
Production coordinated by Greg Nock

To our father.

Without his inspiration, this book would never have been possible.
A part of him lives in every page.
Gracias, Papi. Te extrañamos mucho.

Stamford, Connecticut

Acknowledgments

The original idea for this book was born almost eighteen years ago, so the list of people who helped through the years is extraordinarily long. We'll do our best to keep it short, while trying hard not to forget anyone.

First, we should thank Claudean Wheeler who has been there from the beginning and was there when the first sign was photographed in Cincinnati all those years ago. She was the first person who believed in the concept and pushed us to stick with it. We thank her for that, for her friendship and, of course, for the photography she so graciously contributed.

We'd also like to thank everyone we've met in our travels collecting images: our friends in Venezuela, Japan, Singapore and Spain, but especially Alejandro and Hans in Bogotá, and Teseo and Memo in Mexico City. In addition, we want to thank Lea Girard, Eli Zigdon and Jason Bash for their photographs. For their help, we also acknowledge Alicia Cartenuto, Steven Speeg, ChaChanna Simpson, Tom Barnow, Vincent Ward and Steve Medizabal.

Of course, we thank all the people at HOW Books: Amy, Grace, Megan, Scott and Claudean (again).

Finally, we lovingly thank our mother María Margarita, our sister Erika, the Lutmers, Beth, the rest of our family and friends, and our dogs (Emma and Shampoo) who had to sit in the car and wait while we ran out, snapped a few pictures and ran back before we got a ticket or got hit by a truck.

Kansas City, Missouri

Contents

FLYING
PIZZA
OPEN

MOVED to 26. W. MONUMENT
ROUND THE CORNER TEL 222-8031.
OPEN 10:30 — 7:00 →

Dayton, Ohio

Foreword

INNOCENT MESSAGES

I don't own the alphabet. But I wish I did. Imagine the royalties. When you consider all the people who use those twenty-six letters, even a few pennies a year in payments would add up to gazillions. Sweet.

The truth is, no one owns the alphabet. It's the original open-source software. Anyone is free to pick it up and put it to use. Indeed, that's one of the alphabet's great strengths. The more people who use it, the more valuable it becomes. The same can be said of words and language.

Still, the magic of the alphabet, words and language is so common that we can overlook this miracle. Billions of people can understand my language and recognize the words I write. Even if they are strangers or far away, I can craft a message that will make sense to them. It's astounding that some squiggles on a surface can produce thoughts in people's heads. Sometimes these marks can even make them think, believe or behave in a desired way. This writing is powerful stuff.

It's a miracle anyone can perform. After all, making the shapes of letters isn't hard. Kids can learn to draw a bunch of letters in an afternoon. The shapes are simple. And the level of precision required is very low. Almost any line that goes up, down, up, down will pass for the letter *M*. Only the absolute worst handwriting fails to be understood.

The environments most of us live in are full of written messages. Many of these messages are crafted by professional designers and marketing wizards who work for corporate clients. You see their work every day on TV and in magazines. But our environment is also full of vernacular messages created by ordinary people who haven't studied the niceties of typography and design. People who just have something to say.

Vernacular messages are ubiquitous, and that very fact makes them hard to notice. But if you really look, you'll begin to see plain-talking, hand-crafted and hand-lettered messages everywhere. Look for them on side streets and bulletin boards. There you can see the vernacular messages of the person having a garage sale, the business owner, or the kid who's lost a pet.

These people are trying to solve the same communication problem that professionals face. How can I make my message clear? How can I get people to pay attention? But their approaches can be wildly different. The most interesting ones gallop off in unexpected directions. They are bold, vigorous, innocent, charming, crude, witty, innovative or shocking. Still, they manage to be clear and capture our attention.

This book is full of such examples. Studying them can lead you to more interesting design solutions.

They suggest new ways to organize content, command attention, create surprising juxtapositions, exploit materials and deliver a message—all with almost no budget. In a few cases, the examples instruct by showing what to avoid.

Beyond all that, there's a broader message. Vernacular designs like these remind us that design and clear communication are bigger than any profession can contain. As Tibor Kalman and Kerrie Jacobs wrote in *Print* in 1990, "The vernacular is designed as if design were a regular thing to do, and not the sacred mission of an elite professional class."

The problems our society faces are daunting. Design can help. But if we promote the notion that design is an activity for only learned experts, we're marching in the wrong direction. Design has never been reserved for designers and never should be. The innocent, frisky and peculiar examples in this book are a reminder that, at some level, we are all designers.

Don Moyer
www.thoughtformdesign.com
Pittsburgh, September 2009

1

Detroit, Michigan

By the People, for the People

by Daniel Bellon

Letterforms are truly amazing symbols. One single line—the capital "I" for example—can express thousands of much more complex ideas. In English, it represents the sound "aye." It's the nominative singular pronoun, used by a speaker in referring to himself or herself. In chemistry, it represents iodine; in biochemistry, isoleucine. In metaphysics, it represents the ego; in mathematics it represents the imaginary unit. In physics, it's not only the symbol for an electric current but also an isotopic spin. This single vertical line can be a noun, a pronoun, an affix, a prefix, and an abbreviation. One stroke of a pen or a brush has the power to describe a book's worth of information.

The first Western writing system is generally believed to have been invented in Sumer, by the late third millennium B.C., and developed into the archaic cuneiform. For thousands of years, written communication remained an exclusive engagement between those few who could write and those who could read. Around the 4th and 5th centuries, after the fall of the Roman empire, the only few with contact and knowledge of writing and letterforms in the West were the monks in monasteries in Europe. They copied manuscripts one at a time. As a result, books and reading were so rare that during the Middle Ages, the few books in existence in public libraries had to be chained to shelves and desks to prevent theft. In the 15th century, with the spread of Gutenberg's movable type, books could be mass-produced, and reading became a far more accessible pastime.

Today, it's obviously very easy to encounter type and letterforms in one form or another. You are interacting with type as you read this. Chances are, there are hundreds of other examples of typography around you right now. In modern society, we are bombarded with typographical messages. These messages are received and decoded by millions and millions of literate eyes. But who is delivering the message? Who put the letters together to convey this message? Sometimes they're trained graphic designers, and sometimes they're "amateur designers" who don't have a formal education in typography or design.

What This Book Is Not

These days, anyone with a personal computer can lay out a newsletter and make a sign announcing "Pajama Friday" at the office. This book is not about these signs (Figure 1 on page 4). It's also not about what I call "amateur typographers." These are people who may not be classically trained designers but know a lot about typography, often without being aware of it. Graffiti artists, for example, spend years developing letterforms, the interaction of letters with each other, negative space and other elements in their compositions. As a former graffiti artist, I can tell you these guys take their typography very seriously. They are aware of serifs, counters, ascenders and descenders, kerning, contrast, etc. (Figure 2). Also in this category of amateur typographers are professional sign painters. They are usually trained on the job by older craftsmen and often use their own interpretations of real typefaces. The results are

often remarkable and engaging (Figure 3). These sign painters, too, are aware of type layout, composition, and letterforms. Closely related to them are bartenders, restaurant employees and Starbucks baristas, who change each day's special on a chalkboard. They may not understand the nuances of type design the way graffiti artists and sign painters do, but they develop a certain sensitivity to them if only by sheer repetition, and trial and error (Figure 4). This book is not about those who, knowingly or not, are trained in typography, or those who think they are.

What This Book Is

This book is a celebration of typography and highlights the beauty of typography in its truest form—not as a profession but as a necessity of everyday life. The result may be humorous, unexpected and even charming, but for those who understand the rules that are being broken, these explorations of type design are often refreshing and even inspiring. We want to showcase pieces by the vast majority of people: those who have no knowledge of design, serifs, tracking or kerning and who create graphic design with their hands and break rules they don't even know exist. When people need to communicate, when they need to make a sign to announce a yard sale, they often call up their own creativity and, without the hindrance of rules and preconceptions, they design typography. They use markers, colored pencils, a brush or sometimes unexpected media like electrical tape or cut-out paper. These experiments

Figure 1

Figure 2

Figure 3

in typography are a constant reminder that, even though type and graphic designers often think of ourselves as the keepers of letterforms and typography, we do not own them. Typography belongs to everyone. Typography belongs to the people.

The Story Behind the Book

My brother Klaus and I have been working with type for a long time. As far back as I can remember, we were designing innumerable logos for our imaginary car companies and heavy metal bands. In high school, we had a photocopied punk rock magazine we painstakingly laid out using our father's typewriter, scissors and a stick of glue. So it was a natural progression for us to seek graphic design as a career choice. While attending the University of Cincinnati in the 1990s, I started to pay more attention to handmade signs and found their naive use of typography very interesting. I started photographing them, and I have been collecting images for almost seventeen years. Unfortunately, most of these images have not survived my multiple relocations. Others were taken during the early days

of digital photography and are doomed to remain in the world of 72 dpi for eternity. A few more are trapped in the purgatory that is corrupt files.

When we sat down to pick from the surviving images, I started to notice a few patterns. I noticed that a lot of people treated certain letters in very similar ways. It was a surprise, but a welcome one. I found it interesting and endearing that people from all over the world would create certain letters in the same way. For example, people really like making counters into circles (Figure 5). We also noticed a mixture of upper and lower case in the same word. People seem to love to use a lower case "i" in words that are all uppercase (Figure 6). Also, the thickness of vertical versus horizontal strokes that is second nature to designers is often reversed, creating very odd looking characters (Figure 7). Another interesting observation was the width of the letters "M" and "W." They seem to give people trouble and are usually squeezed to match the width of the letters around them (Figure 8). Sometimes ascenders don't ascend and descenders don't descend. Numbers can be all

over the place. The numbers "2" and "5" tend to be malformed, sometimes to the point of illegibility (Figure 9). The experience has been fascinating, and after all these years we've come to appreciate these mishaps and look forward to them.

In the last five years, when we ramped up our effort to finish the book, collecting photographs became a hunt. The excitement we feel when we see a hand-crafted sign from a distance is indescribable. We take out the camera and take home the trophy of a good photograph for the collection. We quickly learned that most of these signs are found in unexpected locations, making these "hunting trips" quite exciting. We became professionals in the art of spotting a sign while driving at 45 mph, stopping two blocks past it, parking illegally, running back with our camera (which we now carry at all times) and snapping a couple of pictures from a few different angles. Then, after dodging traffic while running back to the car, we start the necessary apologies to our fellow travelers.

Figure 4

Figure 5

Figure 6

Figure 7

Figure 8

Figure 9

Another challenge is the odd reluctance of store owners, shopkeepers and other employees to allow us to photograph signs. We've been yelled and screamed at everywhere, from Harlem in New York City to street markets in Caracas to the suburbs of Hong Kong. In some South American countries, it is illegal to take pictures of buildings, so we have to avoid not only angry and aggressive civilians, but also the often less-than-friendly military police. (It's always a good idea to carry a little cash with you, just in case an officer asks for a donation in order to avoid a night in jail.) We have been all over the world searching for these images, and now we know that the best places to find signs are the less desirable areas of large cities. We skip tourist attractions when traveling. Instead, we spend our time convincing skeptical taxi cab drivers to take us to these places where no foreigner should go, especially when carrying more than a thousand dollars worth of photographic equipment.

In Caracas, a resident of one of these "colorful" neighborhoods took offense to my presence, insisted I leave and threw a brick at me. In retrospect, the dirty looks he'd been giving me since I arrived five minutes prior should have been warning enough. Fortunately for my lack of travel insurance at the time, he missed and I was able to scurry to the nearest subway station and laugh at myself when I realized the photo I was taking was completely out of focus and the incident had been a total waste of time anyway. After that, I was encouraged to hire guides when traveling abroad. A lot of these guys were more bodyguards than guides, really. In Mexico City, after being rushed out of a pretty rough part of the Tepito neighborhood by my guide, I was informed we may have been shot at. *This is great,* I thought, *How could I have explained a bullet wound to my friends and family back home?*

As far as we know, none of the other folks who contributed images for the book were in harm's way, and we are very happy about that. We would never ask anyone to do the silly things we have done or go to the places we have.

It has been a memorable ride, and we are looking forward to a lot more hunting adventures. Hopefully with no shots being fired.

Design and Non-Design Practitioners

by Klaus Bellon

Design is communication. Just as humans cannot *not* communicate (as noted by psychologist Paul Watzlawick), the objects, services and goods we produce are loaded with messages, whether we intend for them to be or not. But are all those who communicate through the objects and solutions they create designers? I strongly believe so. Sadly, most design professionals today would disagree with such a notion. The manner in which professional designers view solutions produced by non-design practitioners has fluctuated wildly between disgust and adoration, the latter often being coupled with an urgent need to document this type of design in order to later co-opt its form. More often than not, the adoration bestowed upon this type of design can best be explained by understanding the way that folk or outsider art has been viewed in the realm of fine art, primarily as an oddity to behold due to the lack of training that the artist has. Much like the bourgeoisie's infatuation with the working class—its values, aesthetics and apparent simplicity in thought—design professionals have idolized these objects for their apparent simplicity. Designers have not, however, taken their creators or intended audience seriously. As such, design professionals often degradingly call such individuals "uneducated," forgetting that we are all designers.

The truth is that design by non-design practitioners (not "non-designers" or the "uneducated") manages to cut through the fog of design movements and formal trends, as well as the realities of client meetings and budgets. This type of design manages to solve problems at a base level, addressing only the primary concerns at hand and, more often than not, communicating with its intended audience very successfully. "Folk design" (a term I will use unwillingly, due to the lack of a more appropriate one) manages to be inclusive in who it communicates with. Additionally, this kind of design manages to communicate a great deal about the person producing the piece of design, as well as her intent. No small feat when one considers that this is exactly what designers who have been trained under the tenets of modernism strive for. Folk design manages to—using scientist Warren Weaver's terminology as put forth in *The Mathematical Theory of Communication*—"deliver a signal from the transmitter to the receiver with minimal noise." This is a significant achievement, considering how seemingly flawed its aesthetic qualities appear to be, an obvious lesson which tells us that clarity in design is not always dependent on formal purity.

From the improvised stool made out of a milk crate and the trash bag used as a raincoat to the hand-painted sign for a roadside business (Figure 1 on page 8), folk design possesses a sincerity and a simplicity that came to all of us naturally before we received a formal design education, whether through traditional means or through intensive work in the field coupled with trial and error.

It's with this in mind that I propose that designers don't dislike and therefore criticize folk design out of a sense of entitlement (though it would certainly appear that way). I also don't believe that designers are wary of folk design because they view themselves as the lone keepers of taste, order and sanity in a world seemingly unwilling to conform to our views of aesthetic perfection. No. The truth, I would like to propose, is even stranger and perhaps more sinister. Designers are all rather envious of the freedom that is afforded to design solutions completed by non-design practitioners. Much like adults who admire the play instincts of a child and long for those days, professional designers long for the ability to communicate simpler messages in a more impulsive, straightforward manner. This is particularly true when it comes to graphic solutions designed by "outsiders" (again, I use this term unwillingly for lack of a better one) to the field.

Of all the forms that folk design could take, graphic communication is perhaps the most common. This is due in large part to the common need we all have to communicate graphically, as well as the relative ease with which information can be shared in this medium. As such, graphic design created by non-design practitioners is perhaps the most abundant and poignant form of folk design around us. It should be noted, however, that folk design exists in almost all areas of design and at all levels of complexity, but it is primarily limited to what Hugh Dubberly refers to as "static" and "dynamic" systems. Dubberly defines static systems as those pieces of design that are not able to act on their own, and consequently have little to no effect on their surroundings. Dynamic systems, on the other hand, can act and thus are able to change their relationship to the environment that surrounds them.

As such, the design systems usually taken up by most non-design practitioners are logical problems for them to tackle, since they are in essence analogous to basic, everyday verbal communication.

Having said that, there is still real value in this seemingly simple way of communicating. The value lies in its honesty and simplicity, but most importantly in its inclusion of a clear point of view and a clear understanding of the intended audience. It's these last two features in particular that are nearly always present in folk design but seldom, if ever, in design produced by many of today's professionals. Understandably, the task of having a point of view and clear understanding of an intended audience is rather simple when the message being communicated is as simple as "Hubcaps" (Figure 2 on page 8), but I must ask: How much more efficiently would a professional design convey this message to its intended audience? More importantly, when the message is intended to communicate to everyone, would a "designed" piece do more harm than good when attempting to communicate such a straightforward message? Considering how our visual landscape is littered with soulless design that appears to be produced by no one, speaks to no one, and consequently excites no one, chances are that a professional's take would not be significantly better.

What is the cause of this design failure? Again, we must go back to our lack of focus and carelessness, which falls in line with what literary critic Wayne C. Booth describes as the "pedant's stance." On the subject of written communication, Booth explains that

this approach consists of "ignoring or underplaying the personal relationship of speaker and audience…." As such, all design can benefit from having a clear sense of its intended audience, and placing great importance on that relationship. If the segment of the population that a piece of design is to speak to is far too broad, audience segmentation and the creation of archetypes within that segment can be helpful in defining the audience. We must look deeper into who our audiences are, remembering all the while that they may be just like us: people, not designers. In doing so, we define our audience, frame our subject matter and find the voice with which we will speak. Can we, as educated designers, learn from those who do not work in the field of design? I believe that we can, but we must at first unlearn. This is particularly true when one considers that the design education many of us have has a strong link to modernist ideology, and thus most of us have a general distrust of any design that does not appear to be pure in its execution or theoretical underpinnings.

Like many other designers who were trained in the United States in the last century, I am clearly aware of the fact that my education was very much a part of the spread of modernist ideology and thought in the American academic landscape. I understand that my proclivity to judge design produced by non-design practitioners is shared by many in the field. As is the case for many others, my professors were trained at places like Yale and the Schule für Gestaltung in Basel, with some going on to work under the tutelage of modernist luminaries such as

Otl Aicher. Though I now realize how common the modernist slant in my education really is, this was not always the case. As a matter of fact, years ago when visiting Bauhaus in Dessau, Germany (perhaps the original cathedral dedicated to modernist thought in academia), I was surprised to see what appeared to be exact replicas of projects I had slowly and methodically worked my way through during the infancy of my design education. These apparent replicas were hanging at the Bauhaus in an exhibition about the accomplishments of its design curriculum. To see those color studies with a name at the bottom that was not mine or one of my classmates' came as a shock to me. I quickly realized that I was part of something bigger. My design education had not suddenly come to exist in an academic vacuum, but was actually part of a long and winding academic narrative. As a result, I was suddenly open to the fact that others shared many of the predilections and tendencies I observed in my work. Similarly, my criticism of some design could also be shared by others as a result of our common academic background.

Today I see and understand that those now-familiar projects are my connection to the beginnings of design education, particularly modernist design. They are experiences that I share with designers across many disciplines, individuals who studied design all over the world at different times in the last century in vastly different environments. Why bring this up? Because this common bond and shared educational background (and its implied theoretical foundations) helps us frame and better

Figure 1

Figure 2

Figure 3

understand the attitudes that most trained designers have about design that is produced by those who are not professionals in our field. It helps us understand the sometimes mocking attitude with which some see this type of design, design that is in some cases characterized as the infantile work of "hacks" who should not dare communicate graphically. Although this type of harsh criticism is usually reserved for untrained designers who attempt to profit from their designs, it is a troubling take on how many view communication by the masses. The other extreme point of view that designers often take regarding folk design can also be seen in those who idolize its form, admiring what they see as its naive visual vocabulary and poor execution. Sadly, neither point of view sees true value in its execution or its inherent connection to its message, when there are in fact some small but valuable lessons to be learned from non-practitioners.

As stated previously, the greatest lesson that this type of design can teach us is its inclusion of voice, tone and clear vision of its audience. It also tells us about the intent with which it was produced, and the fact that it was produced due to a single individual's need to communicate, rather than an institution's need for mass communication. This is an aspect that mass-reproduced, professionally designed objects can seldom replicate. It should come as no surprise that during the 2008 presidential election, numerous reports circulated about signs at political rallies that appeared to be handmade, but were actually mass-produced by traditional printing methods, or

were mass-produced by hand by volunteers (Figure 3). While many were shocked by this slightly dishonest practice, I believe it only served to further show the strength of graphic communication at a personal level. The act (or perceived act) of taking the time to create one's own sign implies that a person truly cares about a candidate or an issue. This is a lesson that all professional communicators should learn from. True passion for a subject is perhaps the greatest tool that we can have at our disposal. Personal involvement leads to better design and more direct communication with our audience. Dishonest or not, political campaigns realized this and attempted to co-opt that sentiment. As communicators, it is our job to understand the message we are trying to communicate and to share our point of view whenever possible.

Designers have seen the value of folk design from time to time, but only partially. During part of the 1980s, and much of the 1990s, a substantial number of prominent graphic designers attempted to rebel from what they saw as the constraints of modernism. One of the formal routes often taken (along with that of distressed typography) was that of looking at the advertising vernacular from previous decades as well as typography and design executed by non-designers in past eras. Sadly, the strongest aspect of such design—intent and point of view—was lost in an attempt to simply copy its aesthetic qualities. Concerned only with the plurality and complexity of its forms, designers who chose to use this visual vocabulary seldom, if ever, chose to connect its

form to a content or point of view, thereby defeating its strength.

Graphic designers have been largely unable to garner genuine interest not only in complexity but also in the meaning of the seemingly banal types of complex design found in places like the Las Vegas strip. In contrast, most modernist thinkers (and those trained by them) have not managed to see the importance or validity of this type of design, and this is to be expected when one takes into account the harsh views expounded by thinkers of the modernist epoch. On the subject of visual literacy and paying attention, design consultant Ralph Caplan wrote, "Visual pollution is harmful not just because it is ugly but because it is distractive. And therefore destructive. Like other pollution, it destroys the balance of nature." While we can generally agree that "visual pollution" can be harmful—if only due to its implied link to other types of pollution (air, water) which we understand and know to be harmful—I think we would be hard-pressed to come to an agreement on just what "visual pollution" is. Is it billboards? Excessive signage?

If you consider the apparent formal imperfections of design as executed by non-designers (Figures 4 and 5), I believe that most examples of folk design would not stand a chance of surviving, should Caplan and thinkers like him have their way. Is this not an elitist and potentially incendiary position for designers to take? Are we, as designers, ready to censor communication in this manner? I don't believe so.

Figure 4

Figure 5

Figure 6

We certainly would not make the same suggestion regarding written or spoken communication that did not suit our tastes in its style and delivery. What makes this even more troubling is that the objection from designers to folk design is formal and does not regard content in any way. What a loss it would be to do away with this type of communication, considering the real ability it has for connecting with its audience, however small or inconsequential its message may seem. It is of the people, by the people and for the people. It may seem odd or a bit unnecessary to think of a message as simple as "Rabits 4 Sale" (Figure 6) as worthy of much thought; however, the way it is expressed says so much about the context in which it was created, the individual who produced it and who it was meant to connect with. As a result, its form cannot be separated from its context, or its author from his intended audience. It is precisely this tight bond that we must learn from and respect, as

it shows us what scholar John Dewey meant when he said, "Receptivity is not passivity." This type of design understands that it is easier for those receiving the message to not only perceive but also recognize its message.

Communication in all its forms and iterations is a crucial part of a fair and equitable society. This is a fact that we have all come to know and understand. A smaller, but no less important fact, is that communication can come in all sorts of mediums, one of which is graphic. Communication by graphic means can and should be executed by all those who feel a need to communicate. If we as designers stand in opposition to this type of communication and expression in any way, even if we only do so to mock or oppose its form, we are standing against the rights and abilities of individuals to communicate, however small or insignificant their message may seem.

Cited Works

Watzlawick, Paul. *Tentative Axioms On Communication from Pragmatics of Human Communication: A Study of Interactional Patterns, Pathologies, and Paradoxes.* W. W. Norton & Company, 1967.

Shannon, Claude and Warren Weaver. *The Mathematical Theory of Communication.* University of Illinois Press, 1949.

Dubberly, Hugh, Usman Haque and Paul Pangaro. "What Is Interaction? Are There Different Types?" *Interactions* magazine, Jan/Feb 2009.

Booth, Wayne. *Now Don't Try to Reason with Me: Essays and Ironies for a Credulous Age.* University of Chicago Press, 1970.

Caplan, Ralph. *Notes on Attention.* Herman Miller, Inc., 1978.

Dewey, John. *Art as Experience.* Perigee Trade, 1959.

Pittsburgh, Pennsylvania

THIS WAY

Arrows and directional signage

Which way? The way the arrow points, of course. The narrowest part is where you insert the videos or the mail, or it points to where you should go. But why? Why shouldn't it be the other way? Maybe the wider part of the arrow is showing us a wider and easier path ahead. We don't really know how this narrow-versus-wide standard was created (maybe from pointing with our fingers, which are thinner than our hands), but we do know it is an international standard.

In all our travels, we never encountered any other device to show direction. The shapes and styles varied greatly, but anywhere we went, we followed the arrows. We may, at times, disregard some social customs, but we never doubt or disobey the arrow.

Green Bay, Wisconsin

Castle Shannon, Pennsylvania

Tokyo, Japan *(Wrong way)*

Pittsburgh, Pennsylvania

Wheeling, West Virginia

Charlotte, North Carolina

FOR ALL YOUR PARTY NEEDS

COLD BEER

VIRGILI DIST.

Bethel Park, Pennsylvania

PULL IN PARKING DRIVE THRU

Atlanta, Georgia

17 W Pharmacy 125 st
Open

Mediciad
Insurance
Accepted

831-0200

Harlem, New York City, New York

Orange, New Jersey

Cleveland, Ohio

Teotihuacan, Mexico

Pittsburgh, Pennsylvania

Denver, Colorado

Dallas, Texas

Pittsburgh, Pennsylvania

Tepito, Mexico, D.F., Mexico *(Clean bathrooms at the end)*

Iztacalco, Mexico *(Bathrooms)*

Dayton, Ohio

Pittsburgh, Pennsylvania

Ossining, New York

Bogotá, Colombia *(Parking - 101 8th Street)*

Sleepy Hollow, New York

Colonia Roma, Mexico, D.F., Mexico *(24-hour public parking)*

Manhattan, New York City, New York

Toluca, Mexico *(Parking $10 an hour)*

Glouster, Ohio

Colonia Doctores, Mexico, D.F., Mexico *(Urgent photos in 5 minutes)*

Detroit, Michigan

Caracas, Venezuela *(Silvia Residence Hostel)*

Tel-Aviv, Israel *(Flowers)*

Chía, Colombia *(Sand and mixed cement depository)*

Pittsburgh, Pennsylvania

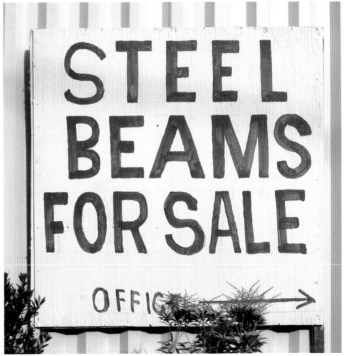

Terre Haute, Indiana

25

Usaquén, Colombia *(Bathrooms)*

Oil City, Pennsylvania

Indianapolis, Indiana

Colonia Roma, Mexico, D.F., Mexico *(Stop suffering, read poetry)*

Colonia Guerrero, Mexico, D.F., Mexico (From top, clockwise: *Library - Pedestrian walkway; Entrance only; Library*)

Long Beach, California

Springfield, Illinois

Pittsburgh, Pennsylvania

White Plains, New York

Bogotá, Colombia *("Arepas" vendor moved one block down)*

Andorra la Vella, Andorra *(Specialty meats)*

Medellín, Colombia

Los Angeles, California

Dresden, Ohio

Pittsburgh, Pennsylvania

The Bronx, New York City, New York

Tlatelolco, Mexico, D.F., Mexico *(J. Pinchardo P. Carpentry)*

Crooksville, Ohio

Buffalo, New York

St. Louis, Missouri

Kansas City, Missouri

Coyoacán, Mexico, D.F., Mexico *(Storefront available - With a room and telephone line - Inquire here)*

Denver, Colorado

OPEN FOR BUSINESS

Advertising and business signage

Few individuals need to communicate more messages more often than business owners. Their signs are crucial: their livelihood depends on messages coming across to potential customers. This is not casual communication. When a business speaks, its owners are trying to get your attention. They want you to come in; they want to you browse… they need you to buy. Although plywood and paint may normally not amount to much, business owners rely on these simple materials as the first step in what they hope will end up in a monetary transaction. Take a look at the following pages to see a variety of creative ways in which owners let customers know what their business is… and that they're open for business.

Bogotá, Colombia

Reading, Ohio

Arroyo Grande, California

Pittsburgh, Pennsylvania

Colonia Tepito, Mexico, D.F., Mexico

Atlanta, Georgia

Ibagué, Colombia *(Automatic car wash - Engine washing - Waxing)*

Toluca, Mexico *(Canine Salon)*

Colonia Doctores, Mexico, D.F., Mexico *(Recycling warehouse - We pick up - Recycling one ton of paper saves seventeen 21-year old trees)*

Manhattan, New York City, New York

Brooklyn, New York City, New York

CARMEN'S

PEREZ

BEAUTY SALON

341-7700

Pittsburgh, Pennsylvania

Manhattan, New York City, New York

Staten Island, New York City, New York

Manhattan, New York City, New York

Bogotá, Colombia *(Photocopies - Replacements)*

Covington, Kentucky

Quito, Ecuador

Caracas, Venezuela *(Premium mufflers - We clean injectors)*

Pittsburgh, Pennsylvania

Washington, D.C.

Cali, Colombia *(Movilcom store - Cellular phone accessories - Sunglasses - Watches)*

Bogotá, Colombia *(Convenience store)*

Bogotá, Colombia *(Sepulveda Bar & Restaurant - Spanish cuisine and tapas)*

Yonkers, New York

48

St. Paul, Minnesota

Mexico, D.F., Mexico *(Parking lot)*

Brooklyn, New York City, New York

Yonkers, New York

Reading, Ohio

Manhattan, New York City, New York

Bogotá, Colombia *(Locksmith - Sales and special promotions - Tools for sale)*

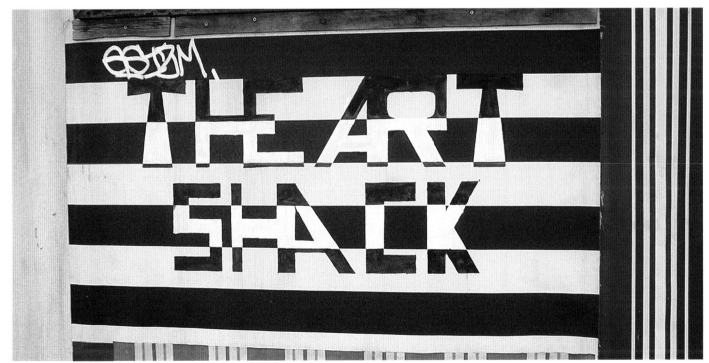

Manhattan, New York City, New York

Providence, Rhode Island

Detroit, Michigan

Harlem, New York City, New York

Mexico, D.F., Mexico *(Rica Birria - Jalisco style "Los Paisas" - Free soup - Plates or tacos)*

Pittsburgh, Pennsylvania

Champaign, Illinois

Manhattan, New York City, New York

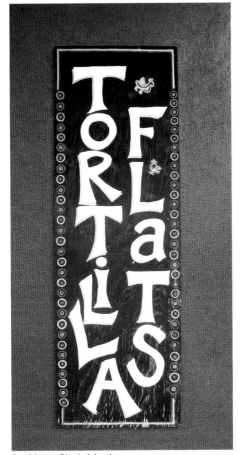

Providence, Rhode Island

Albuquerque, New Mexico

Beechview, Pennsylvania

Pittsburgh, Pennsylvania

Toluca, Mexico *(Engraving - Office supplies)*

Kansas City, Missouri

Mount Vernon, New York

Seattle, Washington

Glouster, Ohio

Pittsburgh, Pennsylvania

Pittsburgh, Pennsylvania

Chapultepec Park, Mexico, D.F., Mexico *(Cameras - Film - Batteries)*

Terre Haute, Indiana

Medellín, Colombia *(Coffee house)*

Seattle, Washington

Seattle, Washington

Ann Arbor, Michigan

Bogotá, Colombia *(Meringue)*

Castle Shannon, Pennsylvania

Harlem, New York City, New York

San Antonio, Texas

Manhattan, New York City, New York

Yonkers, New York

White Plains, New York

Yonkers, New York

Colonia Doctores, Mexico, D.F., Mexico *(Olivos Guitars - Wood crafts - Fabrication, repairs, accessories)*

Yonkers, New York

Medellín, Colombia *(Parking Lot Colombia)*

Medellín, Colombia *(Parking Lot Colombia)*

Mexico, D.F., Mexico *(Flower shop and gifts)*

Manhattan, New York City, New York

Pittsburgh, Pennsylvania

Quito, Ecuador *(Bodywork and paint)*

Toluca, Mexico *(Welcome)*

Bogotá, Colombia *(Lunch, $4000)*

Cali, Colombia *(El Mono Junkyard and Hardware Store)*

Pittsburgh, Pennsylvania

Colonia Roma, Mexico, D.F., Mexico *(Guaranteed turbines)*

Albuquerque, New Mexico

Jersey City, New Jersey

Kowloon, Hong Kong

Toluca, Mexico *(Port of Veracruz Seafood)*

Maracaibo, Venezuela *(My Store - Cold drinks)*

Harlem, New York City, New York

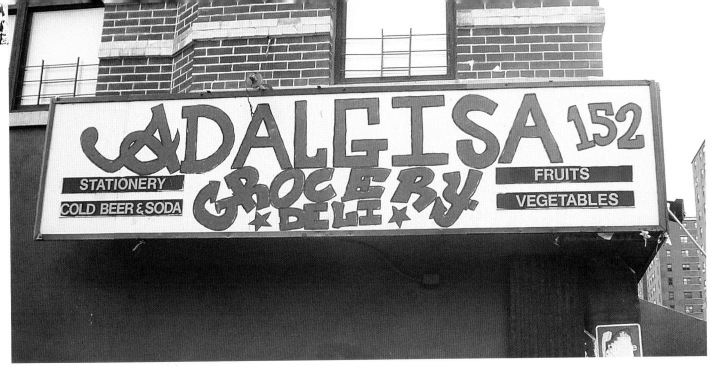

Maspeth, Queens, New York City, New York

Quito, Ecuador *(Since 1998)*

Pittsburgh, Pennsylvania

Bogotá, Colombia *(Calls $200 per minute)*

Kansas City, Missouri

Bogotá, Colombia *(Scaffolding - Stages for events)*

Colonia Roma, Mexico, D.F., Mexico *(Hot sandwiches)*

Nashville, Tennessee

Nashville, Tennessee

the FlYing piZZa

N.Y. STYLE

carry Out

mon. ~ sat.
10:30 am-7:00 pm
Sun. CLOSED

eat in

We serve by the slice.

Dayton, Ohio

Bogotá, Colombia *(Tire changing)*

Bogotá, Colombia *(Tire changing)*

The Best Strawberrie
Are h...

OPEN
O2Amigos
Stand
Strawberrie
AreSweet

Arroyo Grande, California

Arroyo Grande, California

締め切り：

2001年 8月12日

午後5時

御問い合わせ・連絡：

03-4377-0964

03-4377-1588

Tokyo, Japan *(Deadline is 8/12/2001 at 5 PM - For questions call)*

NUMBERS

Prices, phone numbers and other numeric symbols

While our alphabet is of Roman descent, the numeric characters we use are Arabic, an unusual typographic combination that began during the Middle Ages in Europe. Today, when we travel to countries whose languages we may not understand, only those friendly Arabic numbers seem familiar. Will the train we board on this track be inbound or outbound? We're not sure, but at least we know it will be here at 7:30. The elderly woman behind the register greets us, we presume, but it's not until we see the grand total flash over the cash register that we act. Numbers, it would appear, are the only familiar face to greet us during most foreign travel.

Seattle, Washington

Cincinnati, Ohio

Kowloon, Hong Kong

Burlington, Kentucky

Wheeling, West Virginia

Columbus, Ohio

Green Bay, Wisconsin

Carson, California

Orange, New Jersey

Bogotá, Colombia *(Mobile phone cards $150 [per minute])*

Quito, Ecuador

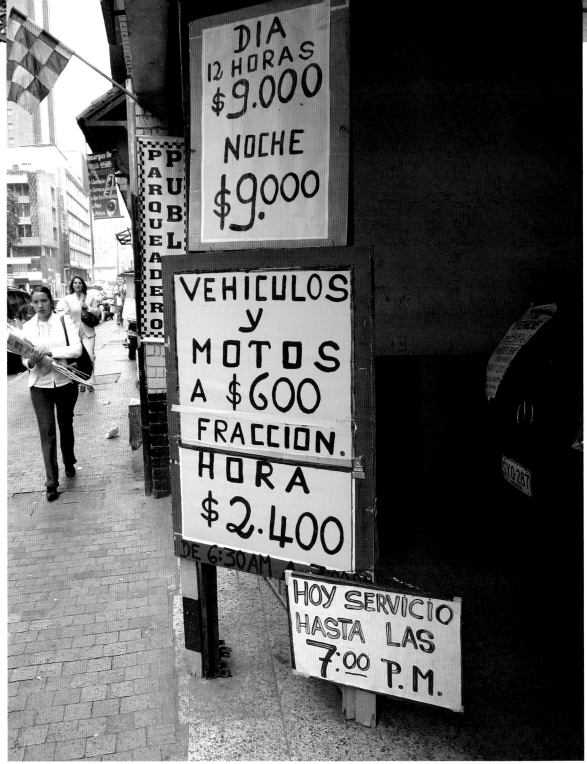

Bogotá, Colombia *(Parking lot - 12 hours $9000 - Cars and motorcycles $600 per hour - Today open until 7:00 PM)*

Denver, Colorado

Pittsburgh, Pennsylvania

OPENING HOURS

MON - 9-30 AM To 9-00 PM.

TUE To SUN - 8-45 AM To 9-45 PM.

நன்றி வணக்கம்

Hong Kong

Wurtsboro, New York

Bogotá, Colombia *(Parking lot - Only driver may enter - Sundays and holidays open until 6:00 PM - Half hour $600, one hour $2400)*

Wurtsboro, New York

Barcelona, Spain

Jerusalem, Israel *(Jerusalem Ice Cream)*

Pittsburgh, Pennsylvania

Kansas City, Missouri

Bogotá, Colombia *(Public parking lot - Vacancy - 15 minutes $600)*

Detroit, Michigan

Jersey City, New Jersey

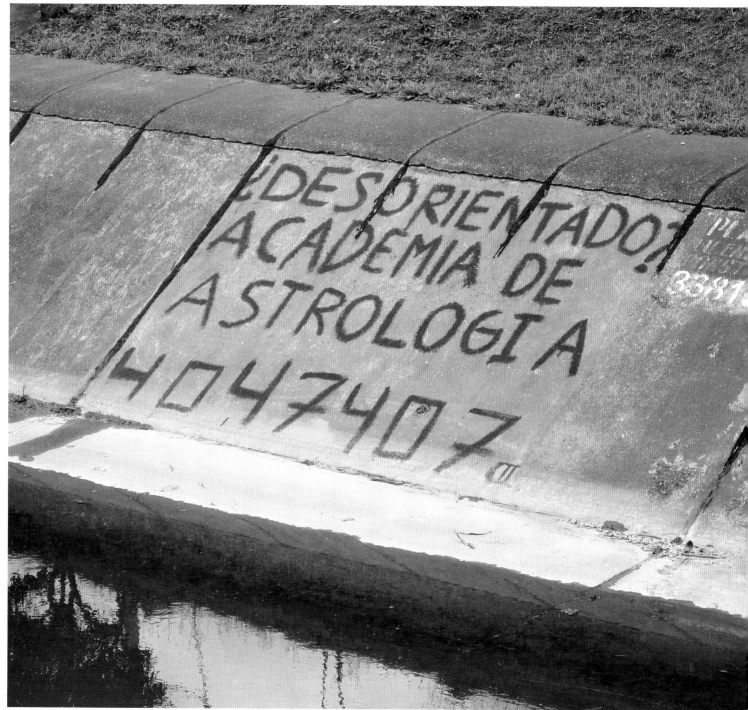

Bogotá, Colombia *(Feeling lost? Academy of Astrology)*

Pittsburgh, Pennsylvania

Quito, Ecuador *(Whole store 25% off - Take advantage)*

Ashtabula, Ohio

Kingston, Jamaica

Chauncey, Ohio

164+/- ACRE FARM
w/STREAM
735·4660

YOUR AD HERE
735·4660

Altoona, Pennsylvania

Caracas, Venezuela *(Autocad blueprints)*

WE WILL SELL ANYTHING ON WHEELS FOR YOU.
CARS·VANS·PICK-UPS·TRUCKS·ETC·
477-3000

Kingston, Jamaica

Kingston, Jamaica

Brooklyn, New York City, New York

Kingston, Jamaica

Chinatown, New York City, New York

Chinatown, New York City, New York

Manchester, Kentucky

Pittsburgh, Pennsylvania

Green Bay, Wisconsin

Rock Creek, Ohio

Medellín, Colombia *(Car wash - $6000)*

Bogotá, Colombia *(Mobile phone minutes)*

Elmsford, New York

Tarrytown, New York

Manhattan, New York City, New York

Bogotá, Colombia *(House of Chinese cuisine)*

Ordino, Andorra

Green Bay, Wisconsin

Harlem, New York City, New York

Colonia Roma, Mexico, D.F., Mexico *(Photocopies - Fax - Repairs)*

Columbus, Ohio

Quito, Ecuador

Chía, Colombia *(This house for sale)*

Pittsburgh, Pennsylvania

Kansas City, Missouri

Dayton, Ohio

Colonia Roma, Mexico, D.F., Mexico

Harlem, New York City, New York

Jersey City, New Jersey

Ardsley, New York

Jersey City, New Jersey

Barcelona, Spain

Chicago, Illinois

Mexico, D.F., Mexico

Tepito, Mexico, D.F., Mexico *(Sale - Genuine watch batteries)*

Toluca, Mexico *(For sale)*

Harlem, New York City, New York

Mexico, D.F., Mexico

Bayonne, New Jersey

Manhattan, New York City, New York

Manhattan, New York City, New York

Mexico, D.F., Mexico *(24-hour hostel)*

Green Bay, Wisconsin

Toluca, Mexico *(For sale)*

White Plains, New York

Quito, Ecuador *(For any questions or service)*

Union, New Jersey

Iztacalco, Mexico, D.F., Mexico *(Complaints)*

Geylang Serai, Singapore

Chapultepec, Mexico, D.F., Mexico *(Sodas and juices)*

Chapultepec, Mexico, D.F., Mexico *(Sodas and juices)*

Mexico, D.F., Mexico *(This house for sale - Parking for small car available)*

Mexico, D.F., Mexico *(Apartment for rent)*

Jefferson, Ohio

The Bronx, New York City, New York

Union, New Jersey

Colonia Guerrero, Mexico, D.F., Mexico *(Service and repairs)*

Manhattan, New York City, New York

Caracas, Venezuela *(Exit - Supermarket)*

PAY ATTENTION

Someone is trying to tell you something

Someone is trying to tell you something, but that person is almost never there. He left behind a sign to alert you. Just as parents childproof their home, we adultproof the world. The messages we convey to others are varied, and the aim is to get their attention. Is this the exit? Is there a bathroom behind this door? In the absence of a human to warn us, typography must inform us. Much like the construction worker who wears a brightly colored shirt while directing traffic, large letterforms and bright colors help convey the tone of the message being passed on. Typography becomes an effective representation of the human voice, each iteration as unique as the person behind its message.

Wurtsboro, New York

Castle Shannon, Pennsylvania

Carson, California

Pittsburgh, Pennsylvania

Pittsburgh, Pennsylvania

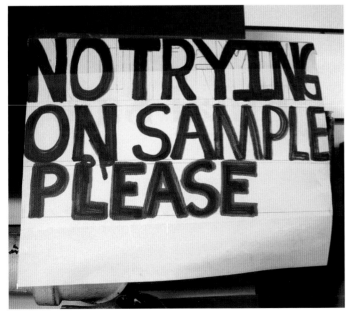

St. Louis, Missouri

Mexico, D.F., Mexico *(Entrance - No Parking)*

MINUTOS

Usaquén, Colombia *(Minutes)*

MUSKINGUM COUNTY
HECKEL RD

Sweet Corn Top of hill Turn left

Muskingum County, Ohio

Detroit, Michigan

Barcelona, Spain *(Don't touch the display case, thank you)*

The Bronx, New York City, New York

Toluca, Mexico *(Polishers)*

Usaquén, Colombia *(Mailbox)*

Spring Hill, Jamaica

San Antonio, Texas

La Massana, Andorra, Tour de France

Erts, Andorra, Tour de France

La Massana, Andorra, Tour de France

Arcalis, Andorra, Tour de France

Arcalis, Andorra, Tour de France

Bogotá, Colombia *(Public parking)*

Brooklyn, New York City, New York

Pittsburgh, Pennsylvania

Villa de Guadalupe, Mexico *(Entrance with balloons is forbidden)*

Tlalpan, Mexico, D.F., Mexico *(Taxi stand)*

Bogotá, Colombia *(Cell phone minutes)*

Bogotá, Colombia *(Desserts and cakes)*

Cleveland, Ohio

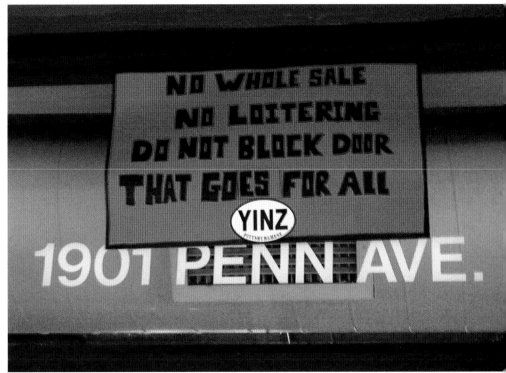

Pittsburgh, Pennsylvania

Pittsburgh, Pennsylvania

Manhattan, New York City, New York

Pittsburgh, Pennsylvania

Mexico, D.F., Mexico

San Antonio, Texas

Barcelona, Spain *(Sale)*

Cincinnati, Ohio

Chía, Colombia *(Mailbox)*

Mexico, D.F., Mexico *(Entrance - Continuous use)*

Manhattan, New York City, New York

Ocho Rios, Jamaica

St. Paul, Minnesota

Brooklyn, New York City, New York

Bogotá, Colombia *(Sale)*

Bogotá, Colombia *(Public bathrooms)*

Bogotá, Colombia *(Paints)*

Brooklyn, New York City, New York *(The garden is open)*

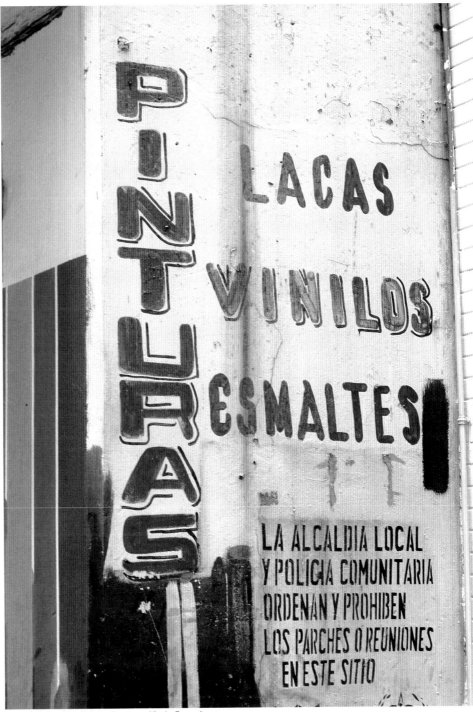

Bogotá, Colombia *(Paints - Lacquer - Vinyl - Enamel)*

x

141

Po Lin, Hong Kong

Bogotá, Colombia *(For rent)*

Toluca, Mexico *(Vacuum cleaners)*

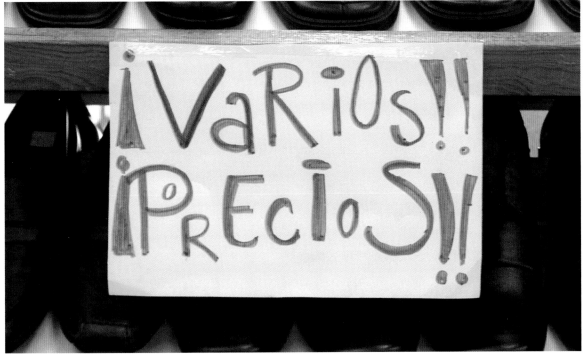

Quito, Ecuador *(Different prices)*

Santo Domingo, Dominican Republic

Mexico, D.F., Mexico

Quito, Ecuador *(Public pay phone)*

Carson, California

Rendville, Ohio

Pittsburgh, Pennsylvania

San Antonio, Texas

Spring Hill, Jamaica

Pittsburgh, Pennsylvania

Spring Hill, Jamaica

Ordino, Andorra *(Private property)*

Usaquén, Colombia

Vail, Colorado

Las Vegas, Nevada

Bogotá, Colombia *(Learn to dance)*

Yonkers, New York

Brooklyn, New York City, New York

Brooklyn, New York City, New York

Long Island City, Queens, New York City, New York

Mexico, D.F., Mexico *(Public restrooms)*

The Bronx, New York City, New York

Jersey City, New Jersey

Pittsburgh, Pennsylvania

Colonia Roma, Mexico, D.F., Mexico *(Public restrooms)*

DIA-DEL-INCENDIO-14-DE-AGOSTO-DEL-AÑO-2000-
PEDI A-LAS-AUTORIDADES-EN-EL-2002-QUE-INVESTIGARAN-
EL-EXP-360-02-DE-LOS-BOMBEROS-DTRO-CAPITAL-HAY-VARIAS-
INFORMACIÓN-DE-PERSONAS-EN-ESTE-EXP-NO-LOS-CITARON-PARA

DECLARAR-PROTEGEN-AL-DUEÑO-DEL-NEGOCIO-TENIA-LA-SANTA-
MARIA-ABIERTA-SALIO-RAPIDITO-Y-AL-INSTANTE-SALIÓ-HUMO-MIS-2-
HIJOS-MENORES-PUDIERON-MORIR-ASFIXIADOS-ESTOS-SEÑORES
LLEVAN-VARIOS-INCENDIOS-EN-SUS-NEGOCIOS-COMERCIALES-
Y-MAFRE-LA-SEGURIDAD-NO-SE-DA-CUENTA-DE-ESTO-AUMENTÓ-
LA-COBERTURA-DE-LA-POLIZA-DIAS-ANTES-DEL-INCENDIO-VAYA-VAYA
Y-EL-FISCAL-NO-INVESTIGÓ-CUANTOS-SEGUROS-HAN-COBRADO-
A-DOS-NADIE-LO-ENGAÑA-EL-ES-VERDAD-Y-JUSTICIA-RECTITUD.
ESC----IA-49-A-METROPOLITANA-EL-CUERPO-DE-BOMBEROS-DSTRO-CAPITAL
COMPAÑIA-DEL-PARAISO-C.I.C.P.C-SOLICITARON-APERTURA-A-ISTE-
NEGO----IO-PIÑATERIA-INVERSIONES-6296-C.A.-AUTORIZÓ-JUEZ-TEMPO
AUA-GONZALEZ-DEL-TRIBUNAL-51-DE-P.I-EN-FECHA-MARZO-20
---05-04-NUEVA-PATENTE-FUÉ-DADA-EN-20-DIAS-VIVA-JESUCRISTO-

Caracas, Venezuela

F.Y.I.

When a few words just aren't enough

Sometimes a few words aren't enough. Sometimes we need a sentence or two (or eleven) to convey our message. Sometimes the content needs to express very complicated ideas, tell a story, give instructions or communicate detailed information. Typography can also convey the tone and purpose of these longer messages, not just its content. A politically- and socially-charged message can't be expressed in just a few words. Today, much is made about our body language, speech patterns and even the facial expressions we make as we speak to one another. Written communication is no different, and it has just as many nuances—all filled with meaning that lets us know more about the information being given.

Cleveland, Ohio

Medellín, Colombia *(Service for home appliances)*

Bogotá, Colombia *(Volunteer fixing pot holes - Thank you for your collaboration)*

Manhattan, New York City, New York

Manhattan, New York City, New York

Pittsburgh, Pennsylvania

Dayton, Ohio

One
Check-cashing
Money Orders
Lottery
Utility Payments

Prepaid Xpress

Stop
Cell Phones
Prepaid Cards
Accessories
Electronics

Shop
Fresh Meats
Deli
Produce
Groceries

Houston, Texas

SUGAR
XL EGG
CHEESE
BACON
COOKING OIL   CAKE

Yonkers, New York

HOT HEROS
ITALIAN
SAUSAGE
CALZONE
CHICKEN
VEAL
BURGERS
EGGPLANT
MEATBALLS
PEPPERSTEAK

Manhattan, New York City, New York

Manhattan, New York City, New York

Bogotá, Colombia *(Printer ink cartridges - Internet - Color copies)*

San Antonio, Texas *(Property of the Mexican government)*

The Bronx, New York City, New York

SLICE OF PIZZA
& BOTTLE OF BEER
OR GLASS OF WINE
★ $6.00 ★ DOMESTIC BEER ONLY
ON PREMISES ONLY

Pittsburgh, Pennsylvania

BLUEBERRY POND
ARTS CENTER
233 CeDar LANe
OSSining. NY
10562

Ossining, New York

Mexico, D.F., Mexico [Sign indicates two areas on the bus route.]

Medellín, Colombia *(Disposable art, gallery and framing)*

Toluca, Mexico *(One glass of juice a day gives you happiness)*

Dobbs Ferry, New York

Yonkers, New York

Pittsburgh, Pennsylvania

AMOEBA MUSIC
CUSTOMER
LOADING AND UNLOADING
ONLY
5 MINUTE TIME LIMIT
VIOLATORS WILL BE TOWED

Los Angeles, California

CEPES 9 30 €
LLAUNA – BOÎTE 1 KG.

TÒFONES 15 grs. 3 90 €
TRUFFRES

ASPERGES 1Kg. 3 60 €
ESPARRECS

Andorra la Vella, Andorra *(Wild mushrooms and asparagus)*

CLUB
PASTOR ALEMAN
LA ROMANA R.D.

La Romana, Dominican Republic *(German Shepherd Club of La Romana)*

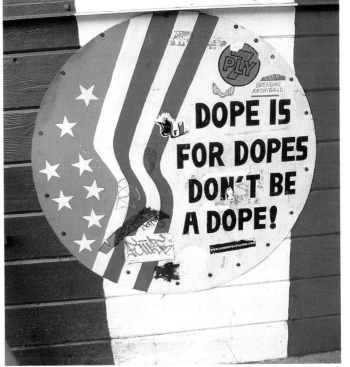

DOPE IS
FOR DOPES
DON'T BE
A DOPE!

Manhattan, New York City, New York

VC CLUB
2132 FORBES Ave.

MEMBERS ONLY...
YOU MUST BE 30
I.D. REQUIRED OR OLDER

LIMITED DRESS REQUIRED
• NO BAGGEY PANTS HUNG LOW
• NO DO RAGS OR HOODS
• NO CAPS WORN BACKWARDS
• PROPER I.D. REQUIRED
• NO DRUGS

ATTENTION MEMBERS
FORMER MEMBERS PLEASE
SIGN UP FOR NEW 2007....
MEMBERSHIPS.
SORRY NO NEW MEMBERS ACCEPTED
AT THIS TIME DUE TO A LIMITED AMOUNT
OF SPACE

Pittsburgh, Pennsylvania

ARREST-A-GUEST
Fur a measly 5 bucks surprise
someone in your gang by gettin'
them arrested. Just fill out
a warrant then we will wrangle
up that varmint and toss them
behind bars. Fur details go to
Trading Post.

San Antonio, Texas

WELCOME
SHAWANGA MOUNTAIN
VFW POST 4947
BLOOMINGBURG •• NY

Bloomingburg, New York

Mexico, D.F., Mexico [Sign indicates two areas on the bus route.]

Mexico, D.F., Mexico [Sign indicates two areas on the bus route.]

Medellín, Colombia [Various dairy products for sale.]

PAN-VIDA
OBLEAS
AVENA HELADA
MASATO
JUGOS NATURALES
CREMA DE CURUBA
POSTRE DE NATAS
ISLAS FLOTANTES
ARROZ EN LECHE
NATILLA DE MORA
LECHE ASADA

Sleepy Hollow, New York

Columbus, Ohio

Barcelona, Spain

Brooklyn, New York City, New York

Pittsburgh, Pennsylvania

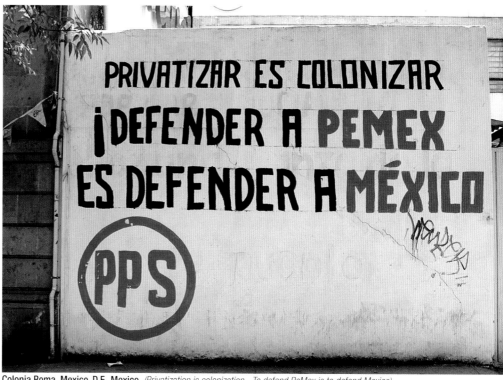

Colonia Roma, Mexico, D.F., Mexico *(Privatization is colonization - To defend PeMex is to defend Mexico)*

Medellín, Colombia *(Hours of operation)*

Ordino, Andorra *(The Bridge d'Ordino was moved on February 15, 1980)*

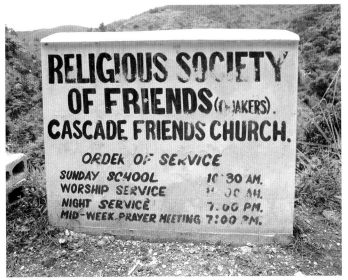

Spring Hill, Jamaica

San Antonio, Texas

Covington, Kentucky

Hastings-on-Hudson, New York

Hastings-on-Hudson, New York

Caracas, Venezuela *(Mobile phone cards for sale)*

Toluca, Mexico *(Carburetor and car computer repairs)*

Bogotá, Colombia *(Photocopies, lamination, computer rentals, mail services)*

Much ado about nothing
William Shakespeare
FREE! Patriots Park

July 30@7:30PM
July 31@10AM 3 7:30PM
Aug. 1@10AM 3 7:30PM
Aug. 2@10AM

Tarrytown, New York

After lot closes at 7:00 pm all remaining keys are taken to the Doubletree Hotel parking garage on the corner of 6th Avenue and Centre Avenue.

THANKS - K7 PARKING

Kansas City, Missouri

1° Piso
LLamadas
Celular $200
Nacional $200
Local $100
Internet $1200
Fax $800
PS2 $1500
XBOX →
$1800
1° Piso

Medellín, Colombia *(Calls - Internet - Fax - 1st floor)*

LIJAS
ESTOPA
CLAVOS
THINNER

Toluca, Mexico *(Sandpaper - Spackle - Nails - Paint thinner)*

Villa de Guadalupe, Mexico [Warning for tourists that begging is prohibited.]

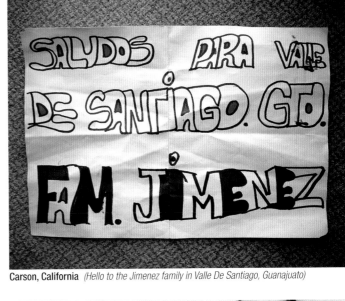

Carson, California *(Hello to the Jimenez family in Valle De Santiago, Guanajuato)*

San Juan, Puerto Rico

Stamford, Connecticut

FONTS

Now you can join the fun, too.

The CD that accompanies this book contains fifteen royalty-free typefaces. We used the typography captured in the pages of this book as inspiration to design all these fonts. In order to make the letterforms seem "un-designed," we had to break rules in typography we have been following for years as professionals, and that challenge proved tougher than we expected. Still, it was a very interesting exercise. Some fonts we based on the media used (such as Electrical Tape or Ballpoint) and others we based on visual patterns we noticed in signs (such as Shadow or Empty). The contradiction and irony of fonts being designed to look like they were *not* did not escape us. We truly hope you enjoy using them.

Ballpoint

The ballpoint pen is one of the most universal writing tools available today. First patented in 1888, this simple utensil has become ubiquitous, as have the signs made by it. Usually thought of as ideal for writing in smaller sizes, users simply create a multitude of lines for use in large-format needs. The line quality, the repetition—even the smudging and bleeding that is common with ballpoint pens—make this font worth celebrating.

NEW! ABCD
EFGHIJ
HUBCAPS KLMNOPQRSTUVWXYZ
NO PARKING! 12345
AREPAS CALIENTES
ONLY $5.25 67890
GASOLINA %!?":\+_*#

Brush

When no proper writing utensils can be found, an old brush will always do. Throughout the world, we've seen brushes used to communicate all kinds of messages. As varied as the messages were, so too were the types of substances used to paint the letterforms. The brushes were often either unbelievably old and in great disrepair, or even homemade. Sometimes, the brush was not a brush at all, but rather a broom of some kind.

GRATIS

PATACONES

GARAGE SALE TODAY

TUNE-UP

DEMOLITION HAMMER

9AM-2PM

FOR SALE, RUNS GOOD

A B C D
E F G H I
JKLMNOPQRSTUVWXYZ
1 2 3 4 5
6 7 8 9 0
%!><?/[]+=

Electrical Tape

An absolute favorite material for making letterforms that we saw time and time again was electrical tape. Who knew that such a seemingly unusual method of writing would be so ubiquitous? Seldom, if ever, did we see duct tape or masking tape used for this purpose. Classic, black electrical tape seemed to be the preferred medium, even if it created obvious problems with curved letterforms.

LOOK

ABCD

EFGHIJ

KLMNOPQRSTUVWXYZ

LEMONADE

CLOSED SUNDAY

12345

BRUNCH

67890

BUY 1 GET 2

CERVEZA Y REFAJO

%!→←?/[]+=

Extended Hollow

Geometric shapes are attractive and can easily make nearly anything seem more orderly and thought out. Unlike the quickly drawn letterforms we found most often, some individuals took their time to map out shapes and widths, even if they weren't always aesthetically pleasing. Perhaps the most interesting aspect of these letterforms was the human element that was always visible: the lines that showed the underlying structure and thought process behind each one.

DON'T
BLOCK DRIVEWAY
FREE TO A
GOOD HOME
BANDEJA PAISA $2500
BATHROOM
OPEN
TODAY ONLY, HALF OFF

ABCD
EFGHIJ
KLMNOPQRSTUVWXYZ
12345
67890
123456789
□/.!>≺ʔ/[]+=

Jen

More often than not, large letterforms amount to little more than people's handwriting, executed through multiple strokes. Due to the tools used for such a task, an inherent variation of widths occurs throughout each letter. How many strokes of the marker will make one letter thick enough? Two, three? Maybe four is more like it.

YES!!

LARGE TACOS

BUY 3 GET 4

DON'T LEAN ON GLASS COUNTER!

REBAJAS

COLD WATER $2

FOR RENT

PANTALONETAS

ABCD
EFGHI
JKLMNOPQRSTUVWXYZ
1234567890!@#$%^&*()

12345
67890
%/.><?()+=

Empty

When confronted with the issue of having to create large letterforms with a thin writing utensil, nearly everyone chose the same solution: hollow letters. In making this choice, less ink is used and letters are drawn quickly. Have you ever tried to fill in a large uppercase *D* with a thin marker? The task can take an eternity, during which you could have created ten signs with simple, hollow letterforms.

USED
TIRES FOR SALE
GLOVES $2.99
BUY ONE
LECHON
ZINES FOR SALE
PLEASE USE SIDE DOOR
PUG PUPPIES!

ABCD
EFGHI
JKLMNO
PQRSTUVWXYZ
12345
67890
%!><?/[]+=

Mercy

Designers often joke about clients wanting them to "make the logo bigger." In practice, we found that many people expressed the immediacy of their message by using large and bold alphabets. Same sentiment, slightly different solution. These extremely bold letterforms would seldom be used by a trained designer, but we found them to be rather effective in conveying the urgency of the message.

REPAIR

BEST PRICES!

TOUCHLESS CAR WASH

USED TRAILER 4 SALE

FREE PIZZA

AGUITA AROMATICA

DONATIONS

CLEAN FILL AVAILABLE NOW

HOT DOG

JUICE, SODA, AND PUNCH

ABCD
EFGHI
JKLMNOPQRSTUVWXYZ
1234567890!@#$%^&*()

12345
67890
%><?[]+=

Old Marker

Sometimes form is simply dictated by the limitations one is given. Certain writing utensils provide obvious limitations and thus can inspire a wide range of creative solutions. After months or years of use, an old marker begins to operate more like a brush, bridging the gap between two widely different writing utensils.

RENT

ABCDEF
GHIJKLM
NOPQRSTUVWXYZ

PLEASE HELP

PARDON OUR DUST WHILE WE REMODEL

FOTOCOPIAS $200

1234

PUMPKINS

567890

INTERNET CAFE

! # $ % < > ˇ

HUEVOS PERICOS CON CHOCOLATE

2 TOPPINGS

[ ] = & * ? /

Serifs

Although handwriting is seldom, if ever, based on existing typefaces, the same can't be said for writing used for more public purposes. The best example we found of this unusual phenomenon was serif letterforms rendered by pens, markers and paintbrushes. Serifs are a result of original stonecutting tools, which were later used in metal and photo type. Today, many people render serifs—which they've seen in digital typefaces—that are actually an iteration of a hand-carved letter from another time and place.

WASH
DOOR 2 DOOR
BUY HERE & SAVE!
LIMONADA
NO HATS ALLOWED
KITTENS
PLEASE, TAKE ONLY ONE
OPEN DOOR SLOWLY

ABCD
EFGHI
JKLMNOPQRSTUVWXYZ
1234567890!@#$%^&*()

12345
67890
%><?[]+=

Shadow

Why would a letterform that has been drawn upon a two-dimensional surface cast a shadow? We're not completely sure, but we know that this effect is common and appeals to people the world over. Light sources are not always consistent, and neither are the length of the shadows, let alone the letterforms. Still, this inventive step—that of imagining the letters as three-dimensional objects—consistently managed to get our attention.

CORN

LEAVE KEYS HERE

DO NOT USE THIS DRAIN!

BANANOS

ONLY $10.99

SPRING SALE

DACHSHUND PUPS

ABCDEF
GHIJKL
MNOPQRSTUVWXYZ

1234
567890

! # $ % ?

Thin
Marker

The distance from which a message will be read must be taken into account for all effective communication. Other than size, the variable most often adjusted in such cases is the overall weight of a letterforms. This font was inspired by the multiple signs we encountered where little care was given to a uniform thickness of the strokes when increasing the weight of the letters.

HAYRIDE

NO CELL PHONES

2X4'S

FRESH CORN

ACEITE

LOADING DOCK→

NO RE-ENTRY

TODAY'S SPECIAL

ABCD
EFGHIJ
KLMNOPQRSTUVWXYZ
!$%-*+\
|;":?/.,=
12345
67890

Lower

Although in our everyday lives we tend to use both upper- and lowercase letters, many signs we saw and photographed seemed to use only uppercase characters. From time to time, a sign had only lower case letterforms, a highly unusual choice. How did someone come to that design decision? We'll never know, but the results are always interesting.

honk

for service please

vendemos alamre por metro, a su gusto

bicicleteria gomez

firewood

brake service

auto detailing + stereo repair

formica sale!

abcd
efghij
klmnopqrstuvwxyz
12345
67890
!@#$%<>"[]=+#()

Square

Most of us default to simple geometric shapes when we need to communicate ideas quickly. So, when creating letterforms, we tend to use more basic, squared-off shapes. Complex curves, as much as they may reflect nature and our own bodies, are cumbersome and require a great deal of finesse to execute. Because of the overall uniformity of the letterforms and the ease with which they can be executed, these square letters are often used for large-scale signs.

FREE

HUB CAPS

NO PARKING

SE VENDE

ONLY $1.99

DON'T WALK!

ABCD EFGHIJ
KLMNOPQRSTUVWXYZ

! $ % – ✳ + \ |
' ; " : ? / . , =

12345
67890

Super Extended

A long and wide writing surface will instantly let an individual know just what type of letterform to design. Utilizing the entire width of the piece of cardboard or wood means creating exaggerated, extremely wide letters. Drawing these types of letters often requires a fair amount of planning, particularly because curves will become distorted with the added width. The answer? Squared-off shapes make drawing these types of letters easier, and thus make communication more effective.

SUNDAY

TWO FOR ONE

$3.00

TODAY!!!

FREE BOXES

EVENT

PARKING

UNICENTRO

ABCDEF
GHIJKLM
NOPQRST
OPQRSTUVWXYZ
1234567890!AT#$%/\+*[]

1 2 3 4 5

6 7 8 9 0

! AT %/ \ + * [ ]

" ' > < ? / \

ABCDEFGHIJKL

Skinny Hollow

The surface on which letterforms are drawn often dictates their shape and size. A short but wide piece of wood will often demand that the characters become extended and wide. If the opposite is true, alphabets become tall and condensed—all in order to make the necessary message fit a given surface.

CHEAP SOFA

HAPPY HOUR SPECIALS

U-PICK

5 STICKERS FOR ONLY $3.99

NO BIKES INSIDE

CEMENTO Y ARENA

ABCDEFGH
IJKLMNOP
JKLMNOPQRSTUVWXYZ
1234567890!@#$%^AND*()

12345678

90><?/"+

%!@()-\|[]+=

Mexico, D.F., Mexico *(Public restrooms)*

Glossary

Ascender
The part of a lowercase letter that rises above the main body of the letter (as in *b*, *d*, *h*).

Baseline
The implied line upon which most typographic characters sit.

Bauhaus
School in Germany that taught design, crafts and fine arts. The school was founded by the architect Walter Gropius, and was in operation from 1919 to 1933. Its teachings became influential in creating modernist points of view in art, architecture, graphic design, interior design and industrial design.

Blackletter
These heavy, black typefaces (whose capital letters are often ornate) were the very first metal type. The earliest of these were from the Gutenberg workshop and were copies of letters found in handwritten manuscripts. Also known as "Old English."

Bowl
The enclosed oval or round curve of letters like *D*, *b*, and *o*. In an open bowl, the stroke does not meet with the stem completely (like the lower bowl in *g*); a closed-bowl stroke meets the stem (like a *q*).

Cap Height
The distance between the baseline and the top of a typeface's uppercase characters.

Counter
Area totally or partially enclosed within a letter. The letters *A* and *D*, for example, have a closed counter, while *S* and *C* have open counters.

Descender
The part of a lowercase letter that descends beyond the main body of a letter (as in *q*, *p*, *j*).

Distressed Typography
Often referred to as "grunge typography," this style of typeface design rose in popularity during the 1990s, and was seen by many as a reactionary move against the clean sans-serif typefaces preferred by modernist designers. Distressed typography became possible due to the availability and affordability of personal computers, which allowed younger type designers to publish their work.

Kerning
Two-dimensional blank spaces between individual typographic characters.

Leading
The spacing between lines of text. The term is derived from the time when printers used actual pieces of lead to increase the spaces between lines of text.

Letterspacing
See tracking.

Sans Serif
A typeface devoid of serifs.

Serif
A stroke at the end of a letterform's main stroke.

Schule für Gestaltung Basel
Highly influential design school in Basel, Switzerland, often referred to simply as the "Basel School." Having been founded by Emil Ruder and Armin Hofmann, the school is often considered to be the birthplace of the Swiss Style of typography.

Signage
Graphic design as applied to indoor or outdoor signs. Signage includes, but is not limited to, wayfinding, neon or lit signs and directional signs.

Swiss Style
A style of graphic design defined by its use of sans-serif typefaces and its heavy reliance on grid systems.

Tracking
The spacing between typographic characters in a body of text. Not to be confused with kerning.

HUB
← CAPS

"BLDG. 4 "CENTERS"
NEW-USED $ ¢ $

CHROM
PACKAG
FOR YOU
TRUCK
CARS

GRILL
OVERLA
DOOR
HANDEL

TAIL/HATCH COVERS
MIRROR COVERS-GAS DOOR
PORT VENTS-TAIL LIGHT B
PILLAR POST COVERS -FENDE
WHEEL SKINS - WHEEL-SIMU
EURO LIGHTS-HITCH COV

Los Angeles, California

About the Authors

Born in Bogotá, Colombia, of German descent, Klaus and Daniel Bellon came to the United States at ages thirteen and seventeen, respectively. Already interested in typography and graphic design and heavily influenced by street art in their native city, the Bellon brothers soon discovered graffiti art in America. They went on to be formally trained in graphic design at the University of Cincinnati's College of Design, Architecture, Art and Planning (DAAP), and have been cataloging and photographing street typography for more than seventeen years.

While attending school, Daniel became a prolific graffiti artist, and to date he has been part of five group shows (two of them in New York) and one solo show in Brooklyn. His art explores typography as an abstract element within the complex compositions of his pieces. As a professional designer, he has worked for two major studios in New York and has been the art director for three publications: *ROBOT*, a magazine about typography and typographic layouts; *THIRDSHIFT*, a graffiti magazine; and *RocketPunch*, a magazine about design and pop art in Japan. His passion for typography earned him a feature in the book *Bodytype* by Ina Saltz. He has received multiple awards, including a Gold Award from the Dayton Art Director's Club. Daniel has designed more than forty typefaces, including a collection of fonts in Japanese. He resides in New York, where he works as an art director for World Wrestling Entertainment.

Klaus is the recipient of five American Graphic Design Awards. He writes about varied topics, including graphic design, music and culture, as well as typography, architecture and cycling. His photography has been featured in several publications, including *RocketPunch* magazine. His professional career has taken him to Pittsburgh, Pennsylvania, were he currently works as an information designer, and he is pursuing a Master of Design degree in Communication Planning and Information Design.

More great titles from HOW Books!

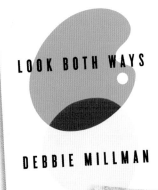

Look Both Ways

In *Look Both Ways*, respected branding consultant and design community leader Debbie Millman has constructed a series of essays that examine the close relationship between design and everyday life. You'll find inspiration on every page as you meander through illuminating observations that are both personal and universal. Each beautifully illustrated essay reveals the magic—and wonder—of the often unseen world around us.

#Z2928, 224 pages, hardcover, ISBN: 978-1-60061-321-0

Written on the City

Written on the City is a glimpse into a vast conversation happening illegally and in public. All over the world, people are writing messages on the walls and sidewalks of the cities in which we live. They are staying up late, breaking the law, and taking risks to say something to you. Some of it is funny. Some of it is beautiful. Lots of it is upsetting, crazy, and brilliant at the same time. And all of it is important. The images contained in this book serve as a global survey of urban typography as they reveal the fears, questions and visions of their creators.

#Z8884, 224 pages, paperback, ISBN: 978-1-4403-0828-4